# Harmony in the Soul:

## The Journey of Stevie Wonder

### Brad W. Flores

All rights reserved. No part of this publication may be reproduced, distributed, or transmitted in any form or by any means, including photocopying, recording, or other electronic or mechanical methods, without the prior written permission of the publisher, except in the case of brief quotations embodied in critical reviews and certain other noncommercial uses permitted by copyright law.

Copyright © Brad W. Flores, 2023.

# Contents

Introduction

Chapter 1: A Musical Prodigy Emerges

Chapter 2: Discovering the Inner Voice

Chapter 3: The Sounds of Motown

Chapter 4: Breaking Barriers: A Message of Equality

Chapter 5: Musical Innovations: The Wonder of Synthesis

Chapter 6: The Songs of Love and Joy

Chapter 7: Musical Evolution: Exploring New Horizons

Chapter 8: Legacy of Inspiration: Impacting Future Generations

Chapter 9: Stevie Wonder: A Life of Resilience and Triumph

Chapter 10: Stevie Wonder's Global Influence

Chapter 11: Stevie Wonder's Musical Innovations

Chapter 12: Stevie Wonder's Enduring Legacy

Chapter 13: Stevie Wonder's Cultural Icon Status

Chapter 14: Stevie Wonder's Musical Legacy: Inspiring Future Generations

Chapter 15: Stevie Wonder's Endless Magic: A Musical Journey

Summary Of All Chapters

# Introduction

"Harmony in the Soul: The Journey of Stevie Wonder" is a captivating exploration of the life, music, and impact of one of the greatest musicians of our time, Stevie Wonder. In this insightful biography, we delve into the extraordinary journey of a musical prodigy who defied all odds to become a legendary singer, songwriter, and multi-instrumentalist. From his early struggles with blindness to his indelible mark on popular music, Stevie Wonder's story is a testament to the power of resilience, creativity, and the human spirit.

With more than five decades in the music industry, Stevie Wonder has crafted timeless melodies that resonate with audiences across generations. This book takes readers on a chronological voyage, beginning with Stevie's humble beginnings in Saginaw, Michigan, and his early encounters with music. We explore his groundbreaking tenure at Motown Records, where he honed his talents, produced chart-topping hits, and became a symbol of the civil rights movement.

Throughout the book, we delve into Stevie Wonder's artistic evolution, from his pioneering use of synthesizers and innovative song structures to his deep exploration of different genres, such as soul, funk, pop, and jazz. We analyze his songwriting process, uncovering the inspiration behind his most iconic songs and the messages he aimed to convey through his music. From love ballads to socially conscious anthems, Stevie Wonder's lyrics have always carried profound meaning and touched the hearts of millions.

In addition to his solo work, we also delve into Stevie's collaborations with other renowned artists, showcasing his ability to seamlessly merge styles and create magical musical moments. From his duets with Paul McCartney to his contributions to the "We Are the World" charity single, Stevie Wonder's collaborations have transcended boundaries and left an indelible mark on the fabric of popular music.

"Harmony in the Soul: The Journey of Stevie Wonder" not only celebrates the musical achievements of this living legend but also provides an intimate look into the personal struggles and triumphs that have shaped his life. From his battles with health issues to his advocacy for social justice causes, Stevie Wonder's story serves as an inspiration to all who face adversity.

Join us on this captivating journey as we uncover the genius behind the melodies, the soulful voice that has touched hearts, and the enduring legacy of Stevie Wonder.

# Chapter 1: A Musical Prodigy Emerges

In the small town of Saginaw, Michigan, a young boy named Stevie Wonder was born into a world of melodies and rhythms. From an early age, it was clear that Stevie possessed a natural gift for music. Even before he could walk, he would tap his fingers on any surface he could find, creating beats and rhythms that hinted at the prodigious talent that lay within him.

Stevie's love for music was nurtured by his supportive parents, Lula Mae Hardaway and Calvin Judkins. They recognized his passion and encouraged him to
explore his musical abilities. At the age of four, Stevie was already playing the harmonica with astonishing proficiency, captivating family and friends with his soulful melodies.

As Stevie grew older, his musical talents continued to blossom. He exhibited a remarkable ear for music, effortlessly playing tunes he heard on the radio or television. His innate ability to mimic melodies and rhythms sparked the curiosity of those around him, and it became clear that he possessed a gift that was beyond ordinary.

Recognizing their son's exceptional talent, Stevie's parents sought avenues to cultivate his musical abilities. They enrolled him in piano lessons, where he quickly excelled, displaying an innate understanding of harmony and melody. Stevie's fingers danced across the keys, effortlessly creating beautiful compositions that mesmerized both his teachers and peers.

Despite his undeniable talent, Stevie faced a unique challenge: he was blind. Born prematurely, he experienced retinopathy of prematurity, a condition that caused his visual impairment. However, this obstacle never hindered his musical aspirations. In fact, his lack of sight heightened his other senses, allowing him to connect with music on a deeper, more profound level.

Stevie's blindness also led him to develop a keen sense of spatial awareness and an acute ability to recognize the smallest nuances in sound. His heightened auditory perception enabled him to discern intricate harmonies, subtle modulations, and complex rhythms. It was as if he could see the music through his ears, painting vibrant sonic landscapes that transported listeners to another realm.

Word of Stevie's extraordinary musical abilities began to spread beyond the confines of Saginaw. At the age of eleven, he was invited to audition for the legendary Berry Gordy Jr., founder of Motown Records. Impressed by Stevie's talent, Gordy signed him to the label, making him the youngest artist ever to join the Motown family.

With the support and guidance of Motown, Stevie embarked on a journey that would propel him to international stardom. His debut album, "The Jazz Soul of Little Stevie," showcased his versatility as a musician, seamlessly blending elements of jazz, soul, and R&B. The album's success paved the way for a series of hit records, establishing Stevie as a rising star within the music industry.

# Chapter 2: Discovering the Inner Voice

As Stevie Wonder's career began to flourish under the guidance of Motown Records, he embarked on a transformative journey of self-discovery and artistic exploration. Chapter 2, titled "Discovering the Inner Voice," delves into the period when Stevie evolved from a young prodigy into a visionary artist with a distinct musical identity.

Motown provided Stevie with a platform to experiment with different musical styles and genres. The label's talented team of producers, songwriters, and musicians collaborated closely with him, nurturing his creativity and encouraging him to push the boundaries of his sound. Together, they embarked on a quest to discover Stevie's inner voice and unleash the full extent of his artistic potential.

During this pivotal phase, Stevie honed his songwriting skills and began to contribute to his own albums. He crafted melodies that reflected his personal experiences, emotions, and observations about the world around him. His lyrics became introspective and thought-provoking, showcasing a depth and maturity that surpassed his young age.

With each new release, Stevie Wonder's musical palette expanded. He experimented with intricate arrangements, incorporating elements of funk, rock, and even classical music into his compositions. The fusion of these diverse influences resulted in a unique sonic tapestry that set him apart from his contemporaries.

One of the turning points in Stevie's artistic journey was the release of his landmark album, "Talking Book." This critically acclaimed masterpiece showcased his ability to seamlessly blend soulful melodies with innovative production techniques. The album's lead single, "Superstition," became an instant classic, topping the charts and solidifying Stevie's status as a musical trailblazer.

As his artistry continued to evolve, Stevie Wonder became increasingly involved in the production process. He meticulously crafted his sound, layering intricate instrumentations and harmonies to create lush and captivating musical landscapes. Stevie's innate understanding of the studio environment allowed him to experiment with new sounds and technologies, pioneering the use of synthesizers and electronic instruments in his recordings.

Beyond his musical accomplishments, Stevie's lyrics began to reflect a deeper social consciousness. He addressed themes of love, spirituality, and social justice, using his music as a vehicle for change and enlightenment. His songs, such as "Living for the City" and "Higher Ground," became anthems of empowerment and resonated with audiences worldwide.

# Chapter 3: The Sounds of Motown

In Chapter 3, titled "The Sounds of Motown," we delve deeper into Stevie Wonder's journey within the legendary Motown Records and the profound influence the label had on his musical development.

Motown, often referred to as "Hitsville U.S.A.," was a hub of creativity and innovation. It fostered an environment where talented artists, producers, and songwriters collaborated, inspiring and challenging one another to create timeless music. Stevie found himself surrounded by a community of exceptionally gifted individuals who shared his passion for excellence.

Within the walls of Motown, Stevie had the opportunity to work alongside renowned songwriters and producers such as Holland-Dozier-Holland, Smokey Robinson, and Berry Gordy Jr. Their guidance and mentorship shaped his artistic sensibilities and refined his musical craftsmanship.

Stevie's tenure at Motown coincided with the label's golden era, a period that produced some of the most iconic songs in popular music history. The Motown sound was characterized by infectious melodies, tight harmonies, and rich orchestration, all of which would leave an indelible mark on Stevie's own musical style.

During this time, Stevie's discography expanded rapidly, with albums like "Up-Tight" and "My Cherie Amour" capturing the essence of the Motown sound. His melodic sensibilities and soulful vocal delivery captivated audiences worldwide, earning him a dedicated fan base and critical acclaim.

Motown not only provided a platform for Stevie's musical expression but also served as a catalyst for his growth as a performer. He honed his stage presence and developed a magnetic charisma that electrified audiences during live performances. With each show, Stevie's reputation as a dynamic and engaging entertainer grew, solidifying his status as one of Motown's brightest stars.

Furthermore, Motown's family-like atmosphere fostered collaborations between artists, resulting in unforgettable duets and collaborations. Stevie's powerful and emotive voice complemented the talents of fellow Motown artists like Marvin Gaye, Diana Ross, and Smokey Robinson. These collaborations produced timeless classics that showcased the synergy and musical chemistry among the Motown family.

Beyond the studio and stage, Motown's influence extended into Stevie's personal life. The label's emphasis on professionalism, work ethic, and social consciousness shaped his values and approach to his craft. Stevie embodied the Motown spirit of excellence, using his music as a vehicle for positive change and advocating for social justice.

# Chapter 4: Breaking Barriers: A Message of Equality

In this chapter, we explore how Stevie Wonder's music became a powerful vehicle for advocating social and promoting equality.

During a time of immense social and political unrest, Stevie felt compelled to use his platform to address the pressing issues of his era. Inspired by the Civil Rights Movement and the fight for equality, his lyrics took on a more overtly political and socially conscious tone.

Songs like "Living for the City" and "You Haven't Done Nothin'" served as anthems for the marginalized and oppressed, shining a light on racial injustice, poverty, and systemic discrimination. Stevie's impassioned performances and heartfelt lyrics resonated deeply with audiences, sparking conversations and inspiring activism.

Beyond his music, Stevie actively participated in events and initiatives that aimed to promote equality. He joined forces with fellow musicians, activists, and leaders in the civil rights movement, using his influence to amplify their messages of unity and justice. Stevie's commitment to making a difference went beyond the confines of the recording studio; he dedicated his time and resources to creating positive change in the world.

Stevie's unwavering belief in the power of music to bridge divides and foster understanding propelled him to reach global audiences. His music transcended boundaries of race, nationality, and culture, forging connections and creating a sense of shared humanity. Songs like "Sir Duke" and "I Just Called to Say I Love You" showcased Stevie's ability to touch hearts and bring people together through the universal language of music.

Moreover, Stevie's activism extended beyond racial equality to include advocating for the rights of individuals with disabilities. As a blind artist, he experienced firsthand the challenges and biases faced by those with disabilities. Through his music and advocacy work, Stevie aimed to dismantle stereotypes and create a more inclusive society that recognized the inherent worth and abilities of all individuals.

# Chapter 5: Musical Innovations: The Wonder of Synthesis

As the 1970s unfolded, Stevie's creative instincts led him to explore the possibilities of synthesizers and electronic instruments. With his insatiable curiosity and inventive spirit, he embraced these emerging technologies, pushing the boundaries of traditional music composition and production.

Stevie's pioneering use of synthesizers added a new dimension to his music, allowing him to create rich, textured layers of sound. He effortlessly blended electronic elements with organic instrumentation, resulting in a sonic landscape that was both futuristic and soulful.

One of the most notable examples of Stevie's mastery of synthesis is his critically acclaimed album "Innervisions." Released in 1973, it showcased his ability to seamlessly integrate electronic textures with his signature soulful melodies. Tracks like "Higher Ground" and "Living for the City" demonstrated his innovative approach to composition, combining intricate synth lines with infectious grooves.

The integration of synthesizers not only expanded Stevie's sonic palette but also enhanced his ability to express emotions through music. The versatility of these instruments allowed him to create otherworldly atmospheres, evoke specific moods, and convey a sense of wonder and exploration. Stevie's intuitive understanding of synthesis as a storytelling tool cemented his status as a true musical visionary.

Furthermore, Stevie's exploration of electronic music extended beyond studio recordings. He brought his innovative sound to the stage, captivating audiences with electrifying performances that incorporated cutting-edge technology. His live shows became immersive experiences, blending traditional instrumentation with futuristic visuals and lighting effects.

Stevie's musical innovations reverberated throughout the industry, inspiring countless artists to embrace electronic elements in their own work. His creative vision and boundary-pushing experimentation helped shape the landscape of contemporary music, influencing genres ranging from pop and R&B to hip-hop and electronic music.

# Chapter 6: The Songs of Love and Joy

This chapter talked about the heartfelt and uplifting music that became synonymous with Stevie Wonder's discography. These songs not only captured the essence of love and joy but also left an indelible mark on listeners worldwide.

Stevie's ability to convey emotions with authenticity and sincerity was unparalleled. His ballads, such as "Isn't She Lovely" and "Lately," embodied the essence of love, resonating with audiences on a deeply personal level. These songs became soundtracks to countless relationships, capturing the magic and vulnerability of human connection.

Beyond romantic love, Stevie's music celebrated love in all its forms. He emphasized the power of compassion, unity, and community through songs like "Love's in Need of Love Today" and "As." Stevie's lyrics and soulful delivery conveyed a profound message of hope and the importance of spreading love in a world often plagued by turmoil.

Furthermore, Stevie's infectious rhythms and upbeat melodies infused his music with a palpable sense of joy. Tracks like "Sir Duke" and "Superstition" had an irresistible groove that compelled listeners to move and uplifted spirits. Stevie's ability to craft music that evoked pure joy created an atmosphere of celebration wherever his songs were played.

Stevie's music became an anthem for generations, resonating across cultural and generational boundaries. His timeless hits continue to inspire joy and spread love to this day. From weddings and family gatherings to dance floors and concerts, Stevie's songs have a way of bringing people together and fostering a sense of unity and positivity.

Moreover, Stevie's positive and uplifting music served as a source of solace during difficult times. His songs became a refuge, offering comfort and reminding listeners of the power of resilience and the beauty of the human spirit. Stevie's ability to uplift souls through his music solidified his status as a beloved icon and a beacon of light.

# Chapter 7: Musical Evolution: Exploring New Horizons

As the years passed, Stevie's thirst for creative exploration led him to venture into uncharted territory, embracing diverse musical styles and genres. He fearlessly incorporated elements of jazz, reggae, gospel, and world music into his sound, expanding the sonic tapestry of his music and captivating audiences with his versatility.

The album "Songs in the Key of Life," released in 1976, stands as a testament to Stevie's musical evolution. It showcased his masterful fusion of various genres, seamlessly blending soulful ballads, energetic funk, and even orchestral arrangements. Tracks like "Sir Duke" paid homage to jazz legends, while "I Wish" showcased his funk-infused grooves.

Stevie's willingness to embrace new sounds and experiment with different musical styles not only showcased his artistic growth but also inspired a new generation of musicians. His eclectic approach to music served as a catalyst for countless artists who sought to break free from traditional conventions and explore the limitless possibilities of musical expression.

Beyond the realm of traditional albums, Stevie's contributions extended to film soundtracks, further expanding his musical horizons. His work on the soundtrack for the iconic movie "The Woman in Red" earned him an Academy Award for the hit song "I Just Called to Say I Love You." Stevie's ability to craft songs that resonated deeply with audiences across different mediums solidified his status as a musical pioneer.

In addition to his musical exploration, Stevie continued to use his platform to address social and political issues. He released songs with powerful messages, such as "Black Man" and "Happy Birthday," which served as calls for equality, justice, and unity. Stevie's music became a vehicle for raising awareness and inspiring positive change in the world.

# Chapter 8: Legacy of Inspiration: Impacting Future Generations

Stevie's artistry transcends generations, and his musical legacy continues to inspire and shape the landscape of contemporary music. Artists from various genres have drawn inspiration from his innovative sound, soulful delivery, and unwavering commitment to social consciousness.

Countless musicians have credited Stevie Wonder as a major influence in their own creative journeys. His ability to blend genres, his mastery of multiple instruments, and his powerful storytelling through music have set a standard of excellence that aspiring artists strive to emulate.

Stevie's impact on the R&B and soul genres is immeasurable. His groundbreaking use of synthesizers, his captivating vocal performances, and his ability to infuse emotion into every note have made him a revered figure among singers and musicians alike. His influence can be heard in the works of contemporary R&B and soul artists who continue to push boundaries and explore new sonic territories.

Moreover, Stevie's commitment to social justice and his use of music as a tool for change have inspired a new generation of artists to use their voices for activism. His songs that tackled issues of inequality, love, and unity have resonated deeply with artists who aim to make a positive impact through their music. Stevie's legacy as an artist and activist has paved the way for artists to use their platforms for meaningful social discourse.

Beyond the realm of music, Stevie's advocacy for individuals with disabilities has sparked conversations and raised awareness about accessibility and inclusivity. His fearless navigation of the music industry as a blind artist has shattered barriers and inspired a sense of empowerment among those with disabilities.

Stevie's music continues to be celebrated and performed by artists of all backgrounds, paying homage to his timeless songs and ensuring that his legacy remains alive. Tribute concerts, covers, and reinterpretations of his iconic hits serve as a testament to the enduring impact of his music on future generations.

# Chapter 9: Stevie Wonder: A Life of Resilience and Triumph

Stevie's life has been a testament to the power of resilience and determination. Born prematurely and with a visual impairment, he faced adversity from an early age. Yet, he refused to let his circumstances define him. Stevie's unyielding passion for music and his innate talent propelled him forward, serving as a constant source of inspiration.

As he navigated the music industry, Stevie encountered obstacles and skepticism. However, his extraordinary musical abilities, coupled with his unwavering work ethic, garnered recognition and acclaim. He overcame industry barriers and shattered expectations, rising to become one of the most revered and influential musicians of all time.

Stevie's personal life also witnessed its share of challenges and triumphs. He experienced heartbreak and loss, but he emerged stronger, channeling his emotions into his music and transforming his pain into soul-stirring melodies. Songs like "Overjoyed" and "Knocks Me Off My Feet" revealed the depth of his emotional journey and his ability to connect with audiences on a profound level.

In addition to personal struggles, Stevie faced societal issues head-on. He became an advocate for social justice, using his platform to address pressing concerns and promote equality. Through his music and activism, he played a pivotal role in shaping the cultural and political landscape, becoming a symbol of resilience and a voice for the marginalized and oppressed.

Throughout his life, Stevie has been recognized with numerous accolades, including multiple Grammy Awards, induction into the Rock and Roll Hall of Fame, and the Presidential Medal of Freedom. These honors serve as a testament to the lasting impact of his music and his enduring legacy.

# Chapter 10: Stevie Wonder's Global Influence

In Chapter 10, titled "Stevie Wonder's Global Influence," we explore the profound impact that Stevie Wonder's music has had on a global scale. From his infectious melodies to his powerful messages, Stevie's music transcends borders and languages, resonating with people from all walks of life.

Stevie's music has a universal quality that speaks to the human experience. His songs, filled with love, compassion, and social consciousness, have touched hearts and inspired change around the world. From the streets of Detroit to the shores of distant continents, Stevie's music has become a soundtrack for generations, transcending cultural boundaries and forging connections between diverse communities.

Throughout his career, Stevie's music has resonated with audiences across continents. His soulful ballads have provided solace and comfort during difficult times, while his upbeat and joyful tunes have brought people together in celebration. From North America to Europe, Africa to Asia, his music has become a unifying force, fostering a sense of shared humanity and cultural appreciation.

Furthermore, Stevie's impact extends beyond his music. His advocacy for social justice, civil rights, and equality has inspired movements and sparked conversations globally. From his participation in the anti-apartheid movement in South Africa to his support for humanitarian causes, Stevie's commitment to making a positive difference has transcended geographical boundaries, igniting hope and inspiring action around the world.

Stevie's influence can be seen in the work of international artists who have been inspired by his music and message. Musicians from diverse backgrounds and genres have paid homage to Stevie Wonder, incorporating his musical sensibilities into their own creations. His influence on global pop, R&B, and soul music is undeniable, and his legacy continues to inspire a new generation of artists to create meaningful, socially conscious music.

Moreover, Stevie's global impact is evident in the countless covers and renditions of his songs by artists from different cultures and languages. His music has been embraced and reinterpreted in various musical traditions, demonstrating its ability to transcend linguistic barriers and resonate with people on a profound emotional level.

# Chapter 11: Stevie Wonder's Musical Innovations

In this Chapter, we delve into the groundbreaking contributions that Stevie has made to the world of music. Throughout his career, he has pushed the boundaries of musical expression, introducing innovative techniques and pioneering new sounds.

Stevie's mastery of the keyboard and his ability to create intricate melodies have set him apart as a true musical genius. His use of synthesizers and electronic instruments revolutionized the landscape of popular music, introducing new sonic possibilities and expanding the horizons of what could be achieved in the studio and on stage.

One of Stevie's notable innovations was his use of the TONTO (The Original New Timbral Orchestra) synthesizer. This massive, custom-built instrument allowed him to explore a vast array of sounds and textures, resulting in the distinctive and futuristic soundscapes that became his signature. Tracks like "Living for the City" and "Higher Ground" showcase the unique sonic landscapes that Stevie crafted through his pioneering use of synthesizers.

In addition to his technical innovations, Stevie's approach to songwriting and arrangement was truly revolutionary. He seamlessly blended genres, infusing elements of soul, funk, jazz, and pop into his music. His intricate compositions incorporated lush harmonies, complex chord progressions, and unexpected rhythmic patterns, creating a musical tapestry that captivated listeners and challenged the traditional norms of popular music.

Stevie's ability to tell stories through his music was another hallmark of his innovation. His albums often had conceptual themes and cohesive narratives, with songs flowing seamlessly into one another. The album "Innervisions," for example, tackled social and political issues, while "Songs in the Key of Life" explored the universal themes of love, joy, and spirituality. Stevie's storytelling prowess elevated his music beyond mere entertainment, making it a powerful vehicle for social commentary and personal introspection.

Furthermore, Stevie's vocal abilities were nothing short of extraordinary. His soulful and emotive delivery, coupled with his incredible vocal range, allowed him to convey a wide range of emotions with authenticity and depth. His vocal improvisations and melismatic phrasing added a dynamic and captivating element to his performances, further showcasing his innovative approach to music.

# Chapter 12: Stevie Wonder's Enduring Legacy

We reflect on the lasting impact that Stevie has had on the music industry, cultural landscape, and the lives of countless individuals. His contributions have shaped not only the sound of popular music but also the hearts and minds of people around the world.

Stevie's music continues to transcend generations, captivating audiences young and old. His timeless hits, such as "Superstition," "Isn't She Lovely," and "Signed, Sealed, Delivered I'm Yours," remain beloved classics that resonate with listeners across different eras. These songs have become part of the collective soundtrack of our lives, evoking memories and emotions that span decades.

Moreover, Stevie's commitment to using his platform for social change has left an indelible mark on society. He has used his music as a force for good, addressing issues of racial inequality, poverty, and injustice. Songs like "Living for the City" and "You Haven't Done Nothin'" have served as powerful anthems, challenging the status quo and demanding a better world. Stevie's activism continues to inspire individuals and ignite conversations about the importance of social consciousness and taking action.

Beyond his musical and social contributions, Stevie's resilience and positive outlook on life have been a source of inspiration. Despite facing personal and professional challenges, he has consistently persevered, reminding us of the strength of the human spirit. Stevie's ability to find joy, hope, and love amidst adversity serves as a powerful example for all of us.

Stevie's influence on the music industry cannot be overstated. He has amassed numerous accolades, including multiple Grammy Awards, induction into the Songwriters Hall of Fame, and a Lifetime Achievement Award. His groundbreaking achievements have paved the way for future artists and shaped the trajectory of popular music.

Furthermore, Stevie's influence extends beyond his own artistic endeavors. He has collaborated with a diverse range of artists, crossing genres and cultural boundaries. His collaborations with musicians like Paul McCartney, Elton John, and Beyoncé have resulted in iconic performances and unforgettable moments in music history.

# Chapter 13: Stevie Wonder's Cultural Icon Status

How Stevie has transcended the realm of music to become a cultural icon whose influence extends far beyond the stage through his artistry, activism, and magnetic personality, he has captured the hearts and imaginations of people worldwide, solidifying his status as a true icon.

Stevie's music has become deeply ingrained in popular culture. His songs have been featured in movies, television shows, and commercials, becoming synonymous with moments of joy, romance, and celebration. From the iconic harmonica solo in "I Just Called to Say I Love You" to the infectious groove of "Sir Duke," his music has become woven into the fabric of our collective consciousness.

Moreover, Stevie's unique fashion sense and charismatic stage presence have made him a style icon. His signature sunglasses, colorful attire, and larger-than-life persona have left an indelible mark on the fashion world. Stevie's fearless self-expression and sartorial choices continue to inspire artists, designers, and fashion enthusiasts to embrace individuality and celebrate personal style.

Beyond his musical and fashion influence, Stevie's impact on society at large is immeasurable. His advocacy for disability rights and his open discussions about his own visual impairment have raised awareness and fostered conversations about accessibility and inclusivity. Stevie has become a beacon of inspiration for individuals with disabilities, proving that determination, talent, and resilience can overcome any obstacle.

Stevie's philanthropic efforts have also contributed to his cultural icon status. Through his involvement in charitable initiatives and his establishment of the Stevie Wonder House Full of Toys Benefit Concert, he has demonstrated a deep commitment to giving back and uplifting others. His generosity and humanitarian work serve as a testament to the power of using fame and influence to create positive change.

Furthermore, Stevie's influence extends to future generations of musicians and artists who look up to him as a role model. His music continues to be studied, emulated, and celebrated by aspiring musicians who strive to capture his essence and carry on his legacy. The impact of his artistry and his unwavering dedication to social causes will continue to shape the cultural landscape for years to come.

# Chapter 14: Stevie Wonder's Musical Legacy: Inspiring Future Generations

Stevie's ability to fuse genres and create timeless melodies has served as a blueprint for countless musicians. His seamless blending of soul, funk, R&B, pop, and jazz has become a source of inspiration for artists seeking to push the boundaries of musical expression. His influence can be heard in the work of contemporary artists who incorporate elements of Stevie's sound into their own compositions, paying homage to his genius while adding their own unique twists.

Moreover, Stevie's impact can be seen in the resurgence of live instrumentation and the appreciation for musicianship in modern music. His commitment to crafting rich, layered arrangements and his virtuosic skills on the keyboard and harmonica have inspired a new generation of artists to prioritize musicality and instrumental proficiency. The organic, soulful quality of his recordings continues to serve as a benchmark for musicians seeking to capture that same magic in their own music.

Stevie's lyrical depth and social consciousness have also left an indelible impact on songwriting. His ability to tackle complex issues and convey profound emotions through his lyrics has set a high standard for meaningful songwriting. His songs have not only entertained but also served as vehicles for social commentary and introspection. Artists today continue to be inspired by Stevie's ability to use music as a platform for social change and personal expression.

Furthermore, Stevie's impact extends beyond the music itself. His unwavering optimism, love-centered messages, and advocacy for unity and equality have resonated with people of all ages. His music serves as a reminder of the power of love, compassion, and resilience, inspiring listeners to embrace these values in their own lives and in the world around them.

As we reflect on Stevie Wonder's musical legacy, we recognize the profound influence he continues to have on the artists of today and the artists yet to come. His innovative sound, meaningful lyrics, and unwavering commitment to his craft have cemented his status as a true musical legend. The echoes of his genius can be heard in the music of contemporary artists, as they carry the torch and strive to make their own mark on the ever-evolving landscape of popular music.

# Chapter 15: Stevie Wonder's Endless Magic: A Musical Journey

Delving into Stevie's musical evolution, tracing the growth of his artistry and the development of his unique sound. From his early Motown hits like "Fingertips (Pt. 2)" to his groundbreaking albums such as "Talking Book" and "Songs in the Key of Life," we witness the artistic progression of a musical genius. Stevie's exploration of different genres, his fusion of musical styles, and his fearless experimentation have resulted in a discography that spans multiple decades and remains timeless.

Throughout his journey, Stevie has gifted us with a treasure trove of unforgettable melodies and lyrics that touch the depths of our souls. From the infectious joy of "Don't You Worry 'bout a Thing" to the introspective beauty of "Lately," his songs have become the soundtrack of our lives, resonating with us in moments of happiness, love, heartbreak, and self-reflection. Each note, each word, carries with it an intangible magic that only Stevie Wonder can conjure.

In addition to his musical prowess, Stevie's ability to connect with his audience on a profound emotional level sets him apart. His performances are transcendent experiences, where he pours his heart and soul into every note, captivating listeners with his soul-stirring voice and impeccable musicianship. Whether on stage or in the studio, Stevie's artistry transcends the boundaries of time and space, enveloping us in a world of pure musical enchantment.

Moreover, Stevie's music has the power to unite people from all walks of life. His universal messages of love, unity, and social justice resonate with audiences across cultures and generations. His anthems, such as "I Wish" and "Higher Ground," serve as rallying cries for positivity and change, reminding us of the transformative power of music to inspire, uplift, and bring people together.

As we conclude our journey through Stevie Wonder's musical legacy, we are left in awe of the boundless magic he has brought into our lives. His unwavering dedication to his craft, his infectious spirit, and his ability to touch our hearts with his music make him a true musical sorcerer. Stevie Wonder's endless magic continues to cast its spell, reminding us of the extraordinary power of music to transcend, transform, and create moments of pure enchantment.

# Summary Of All Chapters

**Chapter 1:** A Musical Prodigy Emerges, chronicles Stevie Wonder's early years, tracing the roots of his extraordinary musical talent and the challenges he faced as a blind artist. It delves into the pivotal role his parents played in nurturing his passion, the development of his exceptional skills on various instruments, and his discovery and subsequent signing to Motown Records. Join us as we explore the emergence of a musical prodigy whose talents would revolutionize the world of music and touch the hearts of millions.

**Chapter 2:** Discovering the Inner Voice, chronicles Stevie Wonder's transformative period of artistic growth and self-expression. It explores the collaborative efforts at Motown that nurtured his creative vision and allowed him to push the boundaries of his sound. From his introspective songwriting to his pioneering production techniques, Stevie's artistic evolution during this phase laid the foundation for the groundbreaking music that would define his illustrious career. Join us as we delve into the inner workings of a musical genius and witness the birth of his unique artistic voice.

**Chapter 3:** The Sounds of Motown, explores Stevie Wonder's immersion in the vibrant and influential Motown scene. It highlights the collaborative nature of the label and the profound impact it had on his musical growth. From the infectious melodies to the dynamic stage presence, Motown's influence permeated every aspect of Stevie's artistry. Join us as we uncover the harmonious marriage between Stevie's innate talent and the legendary Motown sound, paving the way for a musical legacy that continues to inspire generations.

**Chapter 4:** Breaking Barriers: A Message of Equality, explores Stevie Wonder's profound impact as an artist and activist. It delves into the evolution of his socially conscious music, his collaborations with influential figures of the civil rights movement, and his tireless efforts to promote equality and inclusion. Join us as we witness Stevie's transformation into not only a musical icon but also a beacon of hope and inspiration for those fighting for a more just and equal world.

**Chapter 5:** Musical Innovations: The Wonder of Synthesis, celebrates Stevie Wonder's groundbreaking contributions to the world of music. It explores his mastery of synthesizers and electronic instruments, highlighting how these innovations revolutionized his sound and influenced the broader music landscape. Join us as we uncover the awe-inspiring sonic universe created by Stevie's fusion of soul, technology, and boundless imagination.

**Chapter 6:** The Songs of Love and Joy, celebrates Stevie Wonder's remarkable ability to touch hearts and uplift spirits through his music. It explores the timeless ballads and infectious rhythms that have become synonymous with his name, capturing the essence of love and joy. Join us as we immerse ourselves in the transformative power of Stevie's songs and discover the profound impact they have had on individuals and communities worldwide.

**Chapter 7:** Musical Evolution: Exploring New Horizons, celebrates Stevie Wonder's unwavering commitment to artistic growth and innovation. It delves into his fearless exploration of various musical styles and genres, showcasing his ability to seamlessly fuse different sounds into his own unique musical identity. Join us as we witness Stevie's artistic evolution and delve into the vast musical landscape he created, forever pushing the boundaries of what is possible in the world of music.

**Chapter 8:** Legacy of Inspiration: Impacting Future Generations, explores the profound influence of Stevie Wonder on the music world and beyond. It highlights how his innovative sound, social consciousness, and enduring artistry have left an indelible mark on artists who have followed in his footsteps. Join us as we celebrate the lasting legacy of Stevie Wonder and witness the ripple effects of his music across time and generations.

**Chapter 9:** Stevie Wonder: A Life of Resilience and Triumph, delves into the personal journey of a musical icon. It explores the challenges he faced, the triumphs he achieved, and the indomitable spirit that propelled him forward. Join us as we uncover the remarkable story of Stevie's resilience, celebrating his unwavering determination and the extraordinary legacy he continues to build.

**Chapter 10:** Stevie Wonder's Global Influence celebrates the far-reaching impact of Stevie's music and activism. It explores how his universal sound and messages of love, unity, and social change have touched the lives of people around the world. Join us as we witness the power of music to bridge divides, inspire compassion, and create a global community united by the wonder of Stevie's extraordinary artistry.

**Chapter 11:** Stevie Wonder's Musical Innovations, celebrates Stevie's groundbreaking contributions to the world of music. It explores his pioneering use of synthesizers, his boundary-pushing songwriting and arrangement techniques, and his remarkable vocal abilities. Join us as we unravel the musical innovations of a true visionary, witnessing the profound impact that Stevie's creativity and experimentation have had on the evolution of contemporary music.

**Chapter 12:** Stevie Wonder's Enduring Legacy, pays tribute to the profound and lasting impact of Stevie's music, activism, and resilience. It celebrates his timeless classics, his commitment to social change, and his influence on generations of artists. Join us as we honor the remarkable legacy of Stevie Wonder, a true icon whose music continues to inspire, uplift, and resonate with audiences worldwide.

Chapter 13: Stevie Wonder's Cultural Icon Status, celebrates Stevie's enduring influence on popular culture, fashion, and society as a whole.

It explores how his music, style, activism, and philanthropy have elevated him to the status of a cultural icon. Join us as we delve into the multifaceted dimensions of Stevie's iconic status, acknowledging his profound impact on music, fashion, and social consciousness.

**Chapter 14:** Stevie Wonder's Musical Legacy: Inspiring Future Generations, celebrates the lasting impact of Stevie's music on the artists and listeners of today and the future. It explores how his innovative sound, profound lyrics, and unwavering values continue to inspire and shape the trajectory of contemporary music. Join us as we pay tribute to the enduring influence of Stevie Wonder and his remarkable contributions to the world of music.

**Chapter 15:** Stevie Wonder's Endless Magic: A Musical Journey, celebrates the remarkable career of a musical legend. It is a testament to the enduring magic of Stevie's music, his ability to touch our souls, and the profound impact he has had on the world of music. Join us as we pay homage to the one and only Stevie Wonder, the magician whose music will forever enchant and inspire us.

Printed in Great Britain
by Amazon